JOEY GOES TO SEA

JOEY

GOES TO SEA

by

ALAN VILLIERS

Illustrated by

VICTOR J. DOWLING

MYSTIC SEAPORT · THE MUSEUM OF AMERICA AND THE SEA ™

Mystic Seaport
75 Greenmanville Ave., P.O. Box 6000
Mystic, CT 06355-0990

www.mysticseaport.org

ISBN 0-939511-10-X

CONTENTS

Little Joey was a real cat in the full-rigged ship
Joseph Conrad *on her voyage round the world.*
He came from the Solomon Islands, in the
Pacific. Now he lives ashore in a house
in Philadelphia.

I. THE GINGER CAT

EVERY SHIP should have a cat and so the *Joseph Conrad* had one, too. He was a ginger kitten with a very handsome face, a long bushy tail, a bright disposition, and an endless curiosity. He was altogether different from other cats. Most cats in cities either are awfully dirty or else they look as if they owned the world, and when you look at them or talk to them they look back as if you were quite beneath their attention. Not Joey, though. Joey was a sea cat.

He came on board in the Solomon Islands. These are islands in the Pacific named after Solomon's gold because the Spanish sailor who discovered them a few hundred years ago

1

thought they might be the islands where King Solomon had got his gold. But the only thing golden that the sailors of the *Joseph Conrad* saw was Joey the ginger cat. He was golden all over. Even his eyes were gold, and they had a softness in them that did not quite grow out of them even when he was long past kittenhood, and all grown up. His ginger coat was sleek and golden, and the tips of his whiskers were golden, too.

Joey became a sea cat because he happened to be born a few weeks before the sailing-ship anchored off his island. He belonged to Bongo, a big chief on Guadalcanal, which is one of the Solomon Islands. When Bongo saw a sailing-ship anchor off his island, he was surprised, because all the ships

he had seen before were steamers. He went out in his canoe and took the little ginger kitten with him as a present to the crew. Bongo knew that sailors liked cats, and he picked the ginger one because he was so lively and so full of fun. Even before he could see, he staggered about on his stumpy ginger legs and pushed all his brothers and sisters out of the way, falling over and into everything.

The day Bongo took the kitten on board was not so long after his eyes had opened on the excitement of his sunny world. How interesting it all was! He was scared a bit, when he first saw the water, but he soon became used to that, and when he came to the big ship he scampered around and poked his little nose into everything.

The boys of the crew crowded around him and all began yelling at once, suggesting different names for the ship's new cat.

Some wanted to call him Ginger.

"Hey, no!" cried a merry imp named Stormalong. "We've got a ginger chief mate, and that's no name for a cat."

3

"Call him Rufus!" shouted Twitter Thomas.

"Erik the Red," suggested Pete Petersen, the second mate.

"Percy. That's a beautiful name for a cat," said an Australian boy.

"Percy!" shouted the others. "Who ever heard of a cat named that! You might as well call him Claude."

"Or Marmaduke."

4

"Ho, ho, ho, Marmaduke the cat!"

"Erik the Red is not so bad," said Karl. A second mate's suggestions have to be considered, for second mates are important people in sailing-ships. "But what about calling him Little Joey, yes? We name 'im for de ship, no?"

Karl always said "Yes" or "No" after everything just so the others would know what he meant. He was a big German boy with wavy brown hair, a chest like the side of a house and hands like hams. He was boatswain of the *Joseph Conrad.* Boatswains, after second mates, are big people in sailing-ships, and you have to listen to them, too.

His idea for the new kitten's name seemed the best. The boys all spoke of the ship as Little Joey, except when the weather was bad and they called her nasty names, and to think of honoring the kitten with the ship's own name showed that they thought

5

a lot of the little ball of golden fluff that Bongo brought on board.

So "Little Joey" the ginger kitten became. By that time, however, he wasn't there to be named anything, for in the excitement of his christening he had wandered away, and was exploring the ship on his own. By the time the boys decided what to call him, he was nowhere to be seen. He slipped away between Slipey Jones' two big feet and was off on his own.

What a lot he found to see! Never having seen anything very much before, he didn't know quite how strange it was. He walked around to the golden masts and strained his neck looking up to where they reached into the sky, with more and more queer cross-pieces growing out of them and ropes hanging everywhere, ropes and wires and lengths of chain, and canvas neatly furled, and ladders that reached up from the ship's iron sides higher than he could see. Whoever could understand all that confusion? the little cat wondered. Which end of this strange ship went first? He didn't know.

6

But he saw a long strong spar of steel and wood stretching out at one end with sails furled neatly along it, and at the other end was a wheel to steer by. So he guessed that maybe the end with the spar in front went first, and the end with the wheel on it followed along behind.

Not that he cared. He would find out all about everything in good time.

In the meantime he smelled food.

He strolled and scampered round, keen to track down this pleasant smell. He bumped his little carcass against brass guns; he rubbed his fur on a hundred ropes; he climbed up ladders of steel and down wooden ones. He found himself in strange quarters lined with bunks built one above the other, where oilskin coats hung on pegs and big rubber boots were arranged neatly in twenty pairs, in sizes from six to what looked like twelve. He climbed

into one of these and it fell over with him inside so that he had a hard job to get out again, and when he was out he climbed back in and played hide-and-seek with himself for a while. There was nobody else to play with and so he tired of that, and began to chase a ball of twine. That was fun! The ball was about

a mile long, and it rolled all over the place and got entangled with everything, so that long before Little Joey was done with it the boys' quarters were snarled with tarry twine. Then he found a pot of tar, and spilled that; and after that the paint locker provided a lot of excitement.

8

This was a good new home, thought Little Joey—better than any coral island.

He roamed about for hours and always saw something new, and still he had not traced the tempting smell. Away in the front end of the ship, in the bows, he was surprised to come across a sty of pigs. Here three porkers grunted a fat, contented welcome. Joey climbed up on their sty and looked in at them. Ugh! The fat, greasy things lay there in dirt, and the smell that came from them was far from pleasant. Still, they looked friendly enough. Everything about his new home seemed friendly.

Then he met Gus the goat. It should be said that he ran into Gus the goat. Or rather, Gus the goat ran into him. Indeed, Gus the goat butted him.

Gus butted everything except second mates. It was quite

by mistake that he was free. He had chewed through the rope that was supposed to hold him, and there he was, stamping and pawing around the deck, looking for things to butt. He butted Little Joey a good three feet clean in the air. Joey looked around surprised and thought to himself, Hey, what's all this? So he turned twice in the air and landed on his feet, and slapped old Gus with his paw across the nose. Gus was so surprised at that himself that he forgot to butt again, and looked at the ginger kitten with

amazement. What, a kitten slap *him,* the great Gus, Goat of Goats!

Seeing that he had taken the first slap so quietly, Joey walked up and slapped him again.

Then there was trouble. Gus rushed at Joey with lowered head; Joey side-stepped and Gus butted an iron stanchion instead, but he didn't seem to notice that and was after Joey like a flash again. Joey galloped off along the deck, Gus after him with his head down and his tail up in the

air. Joey scampered here and there, slipping round deckhouses, hopping up on rails, dodging the goat, keeping out of reach of the horns.

After a while he saw that this was fairly easy to do, because Gus the goat never looked where he was going. That was why he was such a goat. Gus galloped about and butted into everything, even the coop of chickens

11

on the maindeck aft.   The coop fell over with a crash and all the chickens dashed out, cackling and screeching.   Three of them fluttered up on the side and two fell in the sea, and the boys dived overboard to save them.   Gus bleated and bah-bahed his song of hate; the chickens raised a bedlam of excited noise; the pigs grunted as loudly as they could; the boys shouted and dashed about to save the fowls, Pete and Karl roared orders and Joey dashed into the galley and tripped up the cook who was coming out with a pot of pea soup.   Just at that moment Gus took a flying leap and hit the cook too, and there they all sprawled and rolled in a horrid mess on the clean galley floor—cook and soup and Joey and Gus, all snarled together and mixed up and lashing at one another, the cook with his eyes full of pea soup and Gus bah-bahing and Joey meowing, and the hot slippery soup sliding everywhere.

Gus butted the stove, which was hot, and knocked the coal bin down, and coal scattered all over the already fearsome mess, and Joey was soup and coaldust all over.   Every

12

time the cook tried to rise to his feet he slipped again in the soup and Gus butted him, and Gus got so busy butting the cook that he seemed to forget about Joey. Joey, even in the excitement of it all thought, gosh, this *is* a nice mess. I've got to be friends with the cook; I'll have to blame this on to Gus the goat. So he slithered over the soup and began to climb over the sill of the galley door, to get away.

Just then he became aware of two big cold eyes staring at him, two great big eyes set in a big fat head, with the most enormous cat behind it.

II. JOEY FINDS A FRIEND

HELLO," said Little Joey.

"Hello yourself," said the big cat, in a tone that was far from welcoming.

"I just came on board," said Joey, in the manner of a kitten bent on making conversation.

"I think I can see that for myself," said the big cat, in the manner of a big cat not wanting to make conversation, especially with a little cat that smelled of goat and was covered with pea soup. "I hope you will learn to behave a little better later on," the big cat went on, "and now don't you think you ought to wash behind your ears?"

15

Then the big cat stalked away.

Whew! thought Little Joey. I don't think I've made a friend. Oh well, I hope I can be friends with that big cat, maybe when she gets to know me better.

And Joey sat and thought what he might do to win the big cat's regard. Meeting her like that was bad.

But the big cat was not a bad sort. She was old and big and round, and so fat with eating and from being lazy that she could hardly get out of her own way. Her name was Maisie. Joey heard the cook shouting "Hey Maisie, Maisie!" and the big cat ambled by. He didn't think much of Maisie as a name for a cat, even a she-cat, and somehow his respect for the big fat cat went down a little.

Joey was still an awful mess with soup and coaldust all over him, so Karl the boatswain grabbed him by the scruff of the neck and carted him away to be washed.

"Little Joey, what you been doing?" said Karl. "All covered with dirt and junk and soup, yes? Better we wash your face, no?"

16

"No indeed!" shouted Joey, but Karl didn't understand kitten's language, and he put Little Joey under the pump. Joey kicked and fought, but it was no use in Karl's strong hands.

"Ho ho ho," laughed Slipey Jones, as if it was a very great joke to see a kitten take a bath. He didn't think it was such a joke when Joey shook his wet fur all over him. Joey didn't enjoy the bath himself, but it was better than being covered with soup, and afterwards Karl dried him thoroughly

17

with big towels and put him out to air in the sun. The warm Pacific sun soon dried all the water out, and Joey looked around to see what new mischief he might get up to.

But Karl had thought of that, and the little kitten found himself marooned on the top of a high house in the stern end of the ship, from which the only escape was by climbing the rigging. He sat lazily in the sunshine a while and looked the position over. There was Gus the goat at the other end of the ship busily eating rope, and there was Maisie, slowly licking out the inside of a tin of fish. There was the cook, too, still trying to get his galley clean from all the coaldust and the soup. Away up in the clear blue sky Joey saw brown-skinned boys working on the yards that hung from the masts. They were taking ropes from canvas that was rolled up there, and gradually, as he watched, the kitten saw the big shapes of sails fall loose, to be stretched one upon the other with ropes and wires. He heard whistles blow; boys ran barefoot on the wooden decks, shouting and hauling on ropes. How many ropes there were! Joey thought all

18

the ropes in all the world must be in that ship, and every boy seemed to be pulling on every one of them.

Now he looked up and saw the coconut trees of the lagoon begin to slip by. The ship was sailing. The boys stretched the sails and the wind blew in them, and the ship went along. This was fun. There was no noise and he felt no motion, at first. It was good to be alive and just lie there, lazy and warm and happy.

Joey didn't lie there very long. He wasn't a cat like that. Lying quietly was not his idea of fun.

Besides, he saw some fish skim past. He jumped up when he saw them, and ran excitedly along the top of the house looking for a way to get down.

He noticed a strange thing when he ran up and down. He began to feel funny all over, and his stomach felt as if it were turning inside out inside him. Ugh! That was no good. The ship began to roll and jump about, and Joey felt bad all over. He wasn't very old and he couldn't re-member very much, but he hoped that no matter how old

20

he grew up to be he'd never remember feeling worse than he did just then. He lifted his head and his eyes swam, and his inside began to feel more and more as if it did not want to belong to him.

"Meow," said Joey, in a feeble tone, and he wished that Bongo had left him happily ashore with his mother. It was too late for that, though. There he was, a full-fledged sea cat; and a sea cat he would have to be. He thought perhaps the trouble was that he'd had nothing to eat since he

came on board. Well, there was nothing he could do about that, until somebody took him away from where he was.

Joey sat with his head on his two small front paws, staring at the sea and feeling far from happy.

But what was that he saw? Fish, again, whole schools of them, leaping and skimming over the water. They were the strangest kind of fish. They broke out of the sea in scores and flew, wide-eyed, above the surface, with their great fins extended like wings that shone in the sun, and flew until they fell back, plop-plop-plop, into the water, where big fish with mouths like tunnels waited to gobble them up. What a waste, sighed Joey, and he became so interested watching the flying fish that he forgot all about how badly he had been feeling. All of a sudden he remembered that he was very hungry, and he wished that one of those fish would fly a little higher than the rest and land on board.

Then he saw one fly on board. It rose up, with a flick of its silvered tail, quite close to the ship, and before it could see where it was going, it had shot over the rail like a bullet, and there it was, flapping on the deck.

"Meow!" shouted Joey, meaning that he wanted to be helped down so he could get at the fish. But nobody paid attention.

He didn't shout meow again. He took a run across the top of the house, leapt into the maze of rigging and ropes near by, and slid down to the deck. Then he was on to that fish like a shot out of a gun. Just in time, too, because there

22

was Slipey Jones running with Twitter Thomas after him, both of them intent on being first to catch the fish. Joey slapped the fish with one blow of his ginger paw and gulped it down greedily. Gulp, gulp, gulp, went Joey, and he made fierce noises when the boys came near. He forgot about his table manners and he made horrible noises all the time he ate. That fish tasted good.

No sooner was he through with that one than another came on board, smaller than the first, and Joey leapt at it. He reached it first, too, in front of Slipey Jones, and he was just about to wolf it down when he thought, well, now, I can give this to Maisie. So he dragged it along the deck and brought it to the big cat outside the galley.

23

"Hello," said Joey. "I've brought you a flying fish. They're good, too."

"You're telling me," said Maisie. "I have two for breakfast every day."

But she fell upon the fish with a look almost of affection, and Joey hoped that, in part at least, he might have wiped out the bad impression of the soup.

If he had known how long it would be before the next flying fish came on board, he might not have been so generous. The ship sailed for weeks and not one came on board, though Joey patrolled the scuppers night and morning, and every time he heard a wing flap he was out with his jaws open. But the fish flew by, and the albacore and bonita, those hungry hunters of the sea, ate them.

This all seemed to Joey a dreadful waste. What, fish eat fish? What were cats for?

24

III. OSCAR COMES ON BOARD

THE WIND blew and the sun shone and the ship sailed among the islands, and Joey settled happily on board. He was friends with all the boys, and they were all friends with him. Maisie, after the coldness of their first meeting, paid no attention to him, and he soon learned that he did not need to pay any to her. She lived with the steward and took care of the provision room; all Joey had to do, to stay friends with her, was to keep out of there. That was easy enough.

As for Gus the goat, he ate up so much rope that the crew grew tired of him and they ate him. They ate the pigs too, one by one, and the chickens went the same way.

If there was one bad thing about Little Joey, it was his endless curiosity. Joey thought nothing could be done if he did not look into it. If the boys painted, Joey had to smell the paint; and if he smelled it he got his paws in it, and tramped it everywhere. Then even Karl the boatswain was angry.

"Hey you Joey!" he yelled, "better you leave that paint alone, yes? No?"

So Joey got his tail in it and wiped that all along the varnished brightwork.

Then he went to "help" the sailmaker, and snarled the twine, and got himself rolled up in a bundle of new canvas so tightly and in so many knots that it took half the day to get him out again, and when he was out he rolled up in another one and was almost sewn up in a new mizzen royal,

26

a sail which the sailmaker
was sewing.

"Hey you Joey!" yelled
the poor sailmaker at that,
"leave that canvas alone!"

Joey went to help the car-
penter, and got splashed
with water from the grind-

stone, so he ran away in a hurry. He ran towards the
galley but the cook wouldn't have him in there. The cook
still remembered that wrestle with the pea soup and the coal
and Gus the goat.

So Joey climbed on the chart table, and coiled up there
and slept. He always slept on the chart
table because he got in the way on the
charts. It was not exactly that he loved
being in the way. He was just made that
way. He *had* to get in the way, whatever he was doing. Everybody liked him,

just the same, and if Joey wasn't scampering about in everybody's way they all missed him and looked for him everywhere. Everybody looked after him well, even the cook, in his softe: moments, and Joey's small stomach bulged like a cannon-ball while he grew and grew, and his voice turned gruff and he turned tough, and he learned to climb up the rigging.

At first the steps were too high for him. The boys climbed up the rigging by means of steps of rope tied on both sides, but the steps were about eighteen inches apart and Joey was only seven inches long so he could not stretch so far. But he learned to swarm up the shrouds, with the use of these steps of rope, and soon he always climbed aloft with Karl.

He didn't like going up with Slipey Jones and Twitter and all those noisy fellows, because they mostly went right to the top. He only climbed to the first platform himself,

28

and he liked to sit there looking down at the ship below. He wondered where all that water could have come from, and he wondered, too, when some land would come again and tie up alongside. Sometimes it seemed to him that all the world was water and there was no land, only sea and sea and sea, and the higher you climbed the more sea you saw, but never anything else.

It made Joey feel good to see all that water, when none of it ever wet him.

One day he was prowling along the scuppers, looking for flying fish and whatever else might be around, when all of a sudden, behind a big stanchion, he heard a funny, squeaking noise. He looked around, and there was a bird—a brown bird with white on its wings, and a long beak, and long, gawky legs.

Joey thought of eating the bird at first, and came to get a closer view.

That was a mistake, because the bird pecked him violently on the nose.

"Meow!" screamed Joey.

"Squawk, squawk!" went the bird, pecking away as fast as it could go.

"What's all this going on here?" shouted Pete the second mate, running up, attracted by the noise. "A bird, by gosh!"

"Joey's caught a bird," cried Slipey Jones. "Come on, fellers, here's something new to eat!"

"Go on with you!" spoke up the soft-hearted cook. "You leave that bird alone! If any of you fellows eat that bird, you'll eat nothing more out of my galley."

The poor bird stretched wearily on his long legs, and looked up at all the boys peering down at him.

"What kind of a bird is it?" asked Stormalong. "I've never seen a bird like that."

"It's no sea bird," said somebody.

"How do you know?" everybody else asked at once. "What is there to show that?"

"Well, it hasn't got its sea legs, anyway," said Slipey Jones. "Look at the way it rolls about."

"I reckon it's a frigate bird," said Twitter Thomas. "That's what I reckon."

"Well, that's one sort of bird we know it isn't, then," said everybody else, "because everything Twitter reckons is wrong."

"Oh it is, is it?" yelled Twitter, insulted. "Well, who knows what it is, then?"

"It's a land bird," Pete said quietly. "It's a land bird that has been blown out from some lagoon."

"How could it be blown out, sir?" asked Slipey Jones. "Don't birds know where they're going?"

"Mostly they do," said Pete. "But this must be a young one. Yes, it is a young one," he went on, picking up the bird and examining it more closely. The bird nestled in his big hands and offered no resistance. "It went out too far and was lost, and then the wind blew it here. Lucky for it, it found the ship. Hey, one of you boys fetch some water—and you, Doctor, see if there are any cockroaches in the galley."

"Cockroaches indeed!" said the cook, insulted. Cooks are always called Doctor in sailing-ships, because if they cook the food well everybody is healthy; and if they don't—well, everybody needs a real doctor. "And what, Mister Second Mate, do you think cockroaches would be doing in my galley?" the cook went on.

"I don't know," said Pete, "but if there are any there, this is a good chance to get rid of them."

"I'll go and look," said Slipey Jones, rushing off, but the cook cuffed him over the starboard ear and went off in a huff himself. In a minute he was back, with a score of fat cockroaches on the business end of a shovel. There are always cockroaches in a sailing-ship's galley, in the tropics.

The strange bird gulped greedily at the cockroaches, making short work of them, and it rushed at the water so hastily that it knocked it out of Twitter Thomas's hand, and Twitter jumped.

33

All this time Little Joey looked on intently, wondering why all the fuss was being made over a bird. If only the thing had not had such a long beak, there wouldn't have been any fuss. Then the bird would have been resting securely in Joey's inside. As it was, all he could do was look on and try to make friends with the cook, who was in a good mood to be made friends with, for once, after the cockroach incident. Joey rubbed himself against the cook's skinny legs, and purred. But he wished he had been eating up that bird.

"Let's call the bird Oscar, and make it a pet," suggested Twitter.

"That's a good idea," said Slipey Jones. "It can eat up all the cockroaches in my bunk, anyway."

"All right," said the other fellows. "We'll call him Oscar."

If it was left to me, thought Little Joey, I'd sooner call him a good meal, and that would be the end of it.

34

But that was one thing Joey couldn't interfere with. He had to let Oscar be. He thought that, if they were all going to make such a fuss over him, and he couldn't eat the bird, he might as well pretend to be his friend. So he walked away, to see what else he might butt into. He walked back to the wheel and rubbed himself on the helmsman's feet until the boy shouted "Hey, get away from there! You're tickling me so I can't see where the ship is going."

Then he sniffed at the dial of the patent log, the instrument which measured the speed the ship was making, but it was going round so slowly there was no fun in that. So he coiled up in a clean place in the shade, and prepared to sleep an hour or two.

Joey had not been asleep more than a moment when he heard the lovely sound of a flying fish flapping on the deck.

35

It was so long since one had come on board that he did not recognize the sound at once. When he did, he was up on his feet like a shot.

The fish was a big silver one with pretty blue colors on its back, and it lay in the scuppers opening and closing its mouth, gasping for breath, while it beat on the deck with its tail. Joey's mouth watered at the sight. There was no hurry. No boys were near, since they were all at their navigation lessons, and Maisie was sleeping by the galley-door. Joey scorned to hurry. That fish was his. There could be no doubt about that.

36

That's what he thought, anyway. But just as he came within leaping distance of the tasty fish, Oscar the bird rushed up and gulped it with one mighty gulp. Joey couldn't believe his eyes. To make things worse Oscar stood there looking at him with a wicked grin in his eye, and the tail of the flying fish hanging out of his mouth, still quivering.

Joey thought of all the bad things he had ever heard. The nerve of that miserable bird! Here they go and give him a good home when nobody had ever invited him there and nobody had brought him on board, and he shows his gratitude by eating up a cat's fish! Joey growled and made all the horrid noises he could think of, but Oscar just stood there and grinned, and waved the fish's tail towards him.

That was more than Joey could stand. He made a leap in Oscar's direction, but the tail of that fish disappeared like a flash and Oscar nipped Joey heartily in the ribs.

"Gr-r-r-r," said Joey. "Gr-r-r-r again!"

"Gr-r-r-r yourself," said Oscar, or something like that. "Do you think all the fish in the sea are yours? Well, you'd better be smart about catching them."

Then he grinned, and stood there laughing quietly, wiping away the scales from the side of his long beak on the ropes. After that, he began to walk up and down along the scuppers, peering through the washports and scupper-holes, waiting for more fish to come on board, and Joey looked on sadly. After a while Oscar tired of the exercise, and then he went and stood at one end of the deck in a place from which he could see if any more fish came. Poor Joey could think of nothing better to do than to go and stand at the other end.

There they stood, each at his own end of the deck, waiting for the flying fish to fly on board, Oscar full of fish and smiling to himself, Joey, quite empty, growling.

38

IV. SHARKS!

IT WAS a dull day. The sun shone and the wind was quiet, and the ship drifted slowly. It had rained during the night, and the boys were washing their clothes.

There stood Joey, still thinking of some way to even his score against Oscar. Think as he might—and Joey was good at thinking of things like that—he had never been able to think of anything worse than to push Oscar in a pot of tar, and he'd never been able to get near enough to do that. Oscar's long beak kept him away, and that bird always slept with one eye open. Wherever Joey went, Oscar was watching him. Oscar seemed to have a good idea that Joey was not quite his friend. As for Joey, he found himself wishing that Gus the goat had not been eaten up so soon. It seemed to him that old Gus might have done something about Oscar —butted him in the ribs, for example.

Joey thought and thought, but it did no good. He never even had a chance to push Oscar in a pot of paint.

On this day the ship was going very slowly, so slowly that some big sharks swam astern. Sharks never come near the ship when she is making speed. They are so lazy that the ship has to stop, almost, before they think of swimming up. Which is just as well, usually, because they never do anybody any good. They swim lazily around and eat up garbage and whatever else is thrown over the side, and they wait for boys to fall overboard so that they may eat them.

Joey wished Oscar would fall overboard. They could do without him.

The boys, when they saw the sharks, got a strong piece of rope with a piece of chain on it. They tied a hook on the chain, and threaded a smelly piece of salt beef on the hook. The beef smelled so horrible that it almost made Joey sick, and he wondered that even a shark would bite at such a thing.

But it was no sooner in the water than the biggest of the sharks swam slowly up to it, sniffed at it, turned over on its back, and then, with one great gulp, had that piece of beef three feet down its throat.

Then there was excitement. The shark thrashed the sea with its great tail and its two big fins; little fish which had

been piloting it swam around giving advice; the boys ran aft yelling and shouting; the mate ran along with a blunderbuss and the cook tripped over Maisie in the galley. Maisie, poor cat, jumped for her life, and Oscar ran squawking in the scuppers.

Joey kept his head. *He* wasn't going to be bothered about any shark. You can't eat them, and what you can't eat is never worth getting excited over. At least that was what Joey thought.

The boys tugged and pulled at the heavy rope, and the shark lashed the water and fought to stay in it, writhing, and lunging madly to get the hook out of its mouth. But it was no use. Karl brought a big piece of wood to jam down its throat, and Chips had a bar of iron.

"Yo heave ho, yo heave ho!" yelled the boys, all pulling together, and the shark was pulled up to the rail where Chips hit it on the nose with the bar. Then, with a last strong pull, they had it over the rail. Look out, then! That shark was mad. He leapt and jumped about with his great mouth

42

opening and closing like a giant trap. Joey wondered what he could do to get Oscar inside it, but the bird ran about squawking under everybody's feet and the shark, turning almost a complete somersault, snapped his big mouth horribly close to Little Joey. Joey leapt up, his back arched, and spat. Then the shark rolled towards Oscar and snapped at him. Joey was sorry it missed that time.

The shark was about nine feet long, a big gray one. It smelled badly, and its skin was like sandpaper. Its mouth was full of cruel, sharp teeth, and its eyes were small and full of hatred.

Ugh! Joey was glad when the boys dragged it away to the other end of the ship, to be cut up. They pulled it by very close to him, and again the dreadful thing snapped at him. Joey had enough

44

of that, and this time he ran away up the rigging. There he sat, trying to think of some new scheme to get even with Oscar.

But all he could think of was to let a piece of rope fall down, in the hope that it would land on Oscar, but it landed on Slipey Jones. Slipey looked up and said the most terrible things, and it looked for a while as if he might come running up to give Joey what-for. But he went along to see the shark instead.

After a while, when the excitement was all over, Joey climbed down, and went to sleep on the charthouse table. At least no sharks would come in there.

45

V. JOEY, THE HERO

ONE DAY they came to a funny island. It was just a piece of the ocean with a ring of coral around it.

The ship anchored inside the coral ring, and the boys were sent ashore to gather firewood for the cook.

Joey and Oscar went ashore, too, though nobody invited them. Joey and Oscar never bothered about waiting to be invited. If they weren't asked, why, they came along; and if somebody took them back, they came along again. What could you do with a cat and a bird like that?

Joey sat at one end of the boat and Oscar sat at the other, each with one eye open watching everything around. Most of all, they watched one another.

46

The beach was golden sand, with light jungle growing almost to the water's edge. The boys had no trouble collecting several boat-loads of firewood. Then they built a fire on the sand, in the evening after the day's work, and cooked themselves a supper of shellfish from the rocks, together with some food they had brought from the ship. Joey munched happily on a small fish Karl gave to him, and Oscar stood on one leg with his crop full of herbs and such stuff from the land.

After a while, when they had eaten everything in sight and sung and talked through half the night, the boys slept. Everybody slept, even Oscar. Only Joey sat awake, watching them. There was no sound but the gentle lapping of the water on the sand, and everything was quiet and peaceful. Now and then, a boy stirred or murmured to himself as he slept.

47

Joey drowsed a while.

But what was that? That hissing, rustling noise? That was not water. What could it be?

Joey listened carefully. The strange noise seemed to come out of the sea.

He rose and growled. Whatever the noise was, he didn't like it. His hair bristled. His bushy tail stood out on end. He growled again, looking to see what could be making the hissing noise.

He saw a snake coming out of the sea.

It was a green snake, with yellow bands—a sea snake, from the East Indies, a dreadful poisonous thing with long fangs, which could swim in the sea like an eel and crawl like a snake on the ground. It came nearer, and nearer. Its yellow eyes looked terrible as they caught the glow of the fire, and glinted, and it circled slowly round the sleeping boys.

It circled round and round, leaving a trail of water be-

48

hind it. Joey snarled. The snake hissed and glared. Joey snarled again. Oscar stirred, looked up, began to squawk, thought better of it, and stood there shaking. Joey snarled again louder, and spat. Oscar shuffled towards him for protection. The snake hissed loudly. Joey's hairs stood out on end like bristles on a porcupine, and yellow lights glared in his fiery eyes.

He watched the snake, waiting for a chance to leap on it. The snake watched back, circling slowly and coming nearer and nearer, gradually raising its frightening head.

Maybe if I pretend to sleep again it will go away, thought Joey. Maybe it only wants to see the fire. Perhaps it will go back in the sea.

He sank back on the sand, pretending now to pay no attention to the snake, but watching carefully out of the slits of his half-closed eyes.

The snake stopped. It kept its beady eyes on Joey a long time. He never moved.

Then it peered about.

Like a flash, Joey leapt through the air in one great bound and had that snake by the back of its scaly neck, shaking it. The snake writhed and twisted. Joey held firm. Oscar shrieked. The boys awoke, startled.

"Gosh, what's this!" yelled Karl. He grabbed a big stick from the fire, but he dared not try to hit the snake for fear of hitting Joey. Joey clung on for dear life to the snake's neck, knowing that so long as he held on there he was safe. The snake could not turn and bite him.

"Get a forked stick!" yelled Pete.

"A forked stick," yelled everybody else. "A forked stick to hold the snake down with!"

Everybody yelled and nobody got a forked stick, or anything else, until Slipey Jones jumped into the jungle and came back with two. Karl took one and Pete the other, and they tried to get the forked ends over the snake so that they could hold it down and kill it, without fear of hurting Joey. But the snake twisted so much it was hard to do anything.

Joey still clung on. But he was growing tired.

The snake writhed and flung itself about, beating up the sand with its tail.

"Hey you fellows! Get more sticks! Hurry there!" yelled Pete.

Everybody ran for sticks, but it was not much use. They could not use them for fear of hitting Joey.

51

At length Pete got his fork over the snake's tail and jammed it down into the sand so that the thing could not squirm clear again, and then it was fairly easy for Karl to get his fork over its neck. That was the end, though even then Joey clung on for dear life, and they had to pull him off to get him away. Then everybody belted the snake at once, and it was soon dead.

"Gosh," said Pete. "That was a close call."

"They're poisonous snakes, aren't they, sir?" asked Twitter Thomas.

"You bet your life they're poisonous snakes," said the second mate. "If he had got hold of one of you fellows it would have been just too bad."

"But they live in the water," said Slipey Jones. "I don't understand that. Doesn't the poison get wet?"

"Ha ha ha, listen to that!" laughed the others at Slipey's silly question. Slipey was always asking silly questions. How could a snake's poison get wet?

"It might not have been so funny, though," said Karl, "if old Joey hadn't been awake. No? Good little Joey."

52

He bent over and stroked the little cat's fur, and Joey felt good, sitting there looking at the dead snake and hearing, for once, praise from everybody. Even the cook looked kindly at him, for the moment.

It was some time before they noticed that Oscar was gone. It looked as if the snake had scared *him*. He had run into the woods, and try as they would, they never found him again.

"The sissy," thought Joey. "I knew he was no good. I hope some natives eat him up."

He licked his chops pleasantly at the thought, and was happy to think of all the flying fish that would come his way, now that the bird had deserted. And so at last he went happily to sleep.

53

VI. CAT OVERBOARD!

FOR MONTHS the ship sailed along, and Joey grew big and strong. He slept and ate and played about the decks with his friends, and got in the way of everything and everybody, and pounced on all the flying fish which flew on board, and was contented.

By and by the weather changed.   The sunshine was gone, and the days were wet and gloomy.   The waves tossed high and the ship jumped about in the ocean.   Sometimes the wind screamed in the rigging and there were hardly any sails set, and water came on board.   At such times the ship rolled and rolled until she seemed to be trying to fall over, first this way and then the other.   The pots jumped off the galley stove.

54

Once even a pot of hot water spilled on Maisie and she looked
so sad at the thought of a pot of water doing that to her. As
for Joey, mostly he slept in Karl's bunk, and ate everything in
sight, as usual.

So much water came on board and it rained so often that
it was hard for a cat to get around on deck, and where was
there to go? Joey had been at sea long enough to be used
to a wetting and he wasn't scared, but in weather like that

there really was nothing to do except eat and sleep. He wasn't
scared of the wet or the ocean.

The only time he ever really felt
scared was one day when he fell
in the sea, and that would scare
anybody.

Of course, he chose one of the
worst possible days to do that. It
was quite bad weather.

He was climbing down the rig-

55

ging when the ship rolled heavily, and he slipped. He tried to save himself, but he could not. The first thing he knew, there was the ship sailing on and he was in the sea.

He felt his fur get wet and heavy, and he sank down. He had to fight hard to get to the surface again. Then he struck out bravely, and began to swim. He had never known that he could swim. He'd never had to try before. Now he swam bravely, rising and falling and being thrown up high

as the waves swept under him, trying to keep the salt water out of his nose. He could see now that the ship was stopped. They were getting a boat over the side, to come back for him. He remembered then that he'd not yet had his breakfast that morning. It was Friday—there'd be fish. He had to hurry back on board.

As he swam now he looked up,

56

and there was a big bird coming down to attack him.

Gosh, thought Joey, isn't it bad enough to fall in the sea without having a bird come to eat me?

But it would have to be a very clever bird to get the better of Joey the ginger kitten.

The bird was a big white one, an albatross, with long wings about ten feet across. It came swooping down towards him.

Now, the only thing I can do, Joey thought, is to scare that bird before he has time to take a bite at me. But how could a little cat, swimming in the sea, frighten away a great bird?

The bird swooped down on the kitten, and he lifted a little ginger paw and struck it smartly on the nose. Was that albatross surprised! It was more surprised than scared, if the truth be known, but the effect was the same. It fell in the sea astonished, and sat there staring at Little Joey with a look of amazement. And there it sat while Joey swam strongly by.

Joey, paying no more attention to the bird, looked about to see how they were coming with the boat. They might be doing better, he thought. The trouble with that ship was that there weren't enough cats on board.

He wasn't catching up with the ship very fast, even though it had stopped, and his only hope was that the boat would find him.

His wet fur began now to feel heavier and heavier. He wished they'd hurry with the boat. He didn't know how much more of this he could stand. Swimming around in the ocean, or anywhere else, had never been his idea of fun, or even of proper behavior.

Well, they were doing their best. He knew that. The trouble was it is rather hard to find a ginger kitten in the middle of the South Pacific Ocean.

Joey swam and swam until he was all tired out, and the sea began to get his head down and the salt to wash into his nose. He could not have that. He raised himself again, and struggled on. He trod water a while to get his breath. His legs felt like lead. It began to rain. Funny thing about that rain. There was Joey out in the middle of the sea, wet all over, and yet when it began to rain the first thing he thought of was, gosh, now I'll get wet. He couldn't possibly ever be any wetter than he was, but the rain worried him.

So he swam again, and looked out for the boat. He could see it now, coming towards him, with Karl pulling one oar and Twitter Thomas the other, and Slipey Jones on lookout. But the boat seemed awfully far away.

He sank, and fought back to the surface, only to see those stupid boys in the boat turn and go the other way.

At that he was almost going to give up hope, but he heard

60

a whistle blow on board the ship, and saw the captain point and shout. The boat turned again, and came back towards him. But how slow it seemed. Joey put all his remaining strength into his swimming now. He heard Karl shout, "Come on, Joey! Good old Joey!" He saw the bow of the boat high above him, on the crest of a sea. He felt eager arms reach for him. . . . He remembered no more.

He came to in the warmth of the dry galley, with a tin of fish lying open beside him and big Maisie licking the salt out of the back of his neck.

61

"Hey Maisie, do you think I am a sissy, or something?" said Joey.

But he was pleased, just the same; and even more pleased with the tin of fish.

Next day he was climbing round the rigging again.   You couldn't scare Little Joey!   But Pete the second mate saw him and was afraid he might fall in the ocean.

"Hey you Joey!" he shouted up, "Come on down from there.   We're not going back for you twice!"

62

VII. THE END OF THE VOYAGE

IF ALL voyagings have beginnings they must also end, and one day the ship came into a port and did not go out again.

It was a big, noisy port, with many ships and thousands upon thousands of people.

The ship was sold, and the boys left, and went home. Pete left, and Karl, and the cook, who took Maisie away with him, and after a while Joey was left there alone. Karl wanted to take him home and so did Pete, but Joey liked better to stay with the ship for she was the only home he knew. He had no place to go, and the old night watchman looked after him, putting out his plate of milk and his tin of fish every morning.

63

It began to be cold, and it was not nice on board any longer. One day a lady came from Philadelphia, and she took Joey away down there to give him a home. Joey had to go, because he could not quarrel with a lady, but he hated the idea of leaving the ship. The trip to Philadelphia in the train was very frightening, and the town itself was big and noisy. But it was better than the docks, and in the course of time Joey grew almost to like it. His new friends were so kind to him that he could not help liking them, and he had a lovely home.

64

But he always remembered the ship and the sea, and he often wished that he were back there, sailing.

The last I heard of Joey some painters came to the house for the spring-cleaning. They brought big ladders with them, and as soon as he saw them put the ladders up Joey became very excited. They reminded him of the rigging of the ship he knew so well, and as soon as they were up he took one happy leap and climbed to the top.

There he scampered about and jumped and had good fun, and he looked all around, pretending to be keeping lookout for flying fish.

But the painters were scared that he would fall down, and hurt himself.

"Hey cat!" they yelled, "Get down from there! You'll break your neck!"

Break his neck, indeed! Joey was insulted. What did they think he was? He could show them something about climbing as it really should be done, if there was anything to climb on. Ladders, huh—they were for sissies and such.

So he knocked down a pail of paint, and jumped at one of the painters so suddenly that the painter got the shock of his life, and tore out into the street with Joey after him.

For all I know, perhaps that painter is still running, with Little Joey after him. And if he ever catches up, it will be too bad!

Joseph and Conrad on the deck of the *Joseph Conrad*. Photo by Hans Christian Petersen. (Zangenberg Collection, Mystic Seaport, 1988-10-284)

AFTERWORD

This is a true story—maybe a little simpler than what really happened, and with some names changed, but Joey was real and really did these things.

The author, Alan Villiers, was in his early 30s when he realized his dream of sailing around the world with about 20 young people to show them the values to be learned as part of a sailing-ship crew. An Australian, Villiers had made six voyages in sailing ships carrying grain from Australia to Europe and had sailed and whaled in Australian waters. In 1934 he learned that the 100-foot, square-rigged ship *Georg Stage* was up for sale.

Launched in 1882, the little Danish ship had been designed to carry 80 boys on summer training cruises to prepare them for life at sea. Well built of iron, and very seaworthy, the ship met only one bad accident during her 50 years of service. One night in 1905 a steamship ran into the *Georg Stage*, sinking her with the loss of 22 cadets. To make her as safe and unsinkable as a sailing ship could be, she was repaired with four watertight bulkheads.

Villiers bought the ship, sailed her from Denmark to England, and renamed her *Joseph Conrad* in honor of the famous sailor and author of sea fiction. He took aboard a crew of sailors, including the 36-year-old cook W.A. Catchpole, and paying teenage cadets, including "Stormalong," who was 15-year-old Stanley Goodchild. The "Twitter Thomas" and "Slipey Jones" in this book are made-up names.

The *Joseph Conrad* sailed from England in October 1934 and arrived at New York in December. A storm put her on the rocks there, but she was repaired and sailed to Rio de Janeiro, Brazil, then across the South Atlantic to Cape Town, South Africa, and on across the Indian Ocean. She swung through the islands of Indonesia and the Philippines before arriving in the Solomon Islands, northeast of New Guinea in the South Pacific.

Joey's world: the *Joseph Conrad* at sea. Photo by Hans Christian Petersen, (Zangenberg Collection, Mystic Seaport, 1988-10-111)

Early in November 1935 the little ship anchored at Berande on Guadalcanal in the Solomon Islands. After the crew had a very pleasant visit, the natives presented them with two kittens, which must have been descended from some ships' cats that had been left at the island in earlier times. The ship's new kittens were christened Joseph and Conrad.

The ginger cat, Joseph, was more adventurous and became the favorite among the crew. "He was accustomed to mount to the maintop each morning, springing gaily up the shrouds, and from that height surveying imperiously what he doubtless regarded as his domain," wrote Alan Villiers in his account of the voyage, *Cruise of the Conrad*. To simplify his story, Villiers did not mention Conrad in this book.

Sailors have always been afraid of sharks and sea snakes. That is why the *Joseph Conrad*'s crew was so quick to kill the ones they encountered, as described in this book. Today we might be equally frightened, but perhaps more willing just to watch these unique creatures.

With Joey on board, the ship sailed south to Australia, crossed to New Zealand, and returned to the eastern tip of New Guinea to deliver some mining prospectors. On nearby Wari Island the ship drifted onto the coral reef. At first it stuck fast, but working frantically the crew was finally able to haul the *Conrad* free. Escaping from the dangerous Coral Sea, the ship sailed back toward Australia, then passed between the islands of New Zealand on its way eastward.

On May 22, 1936, as the ship rolled through stormy seas east of New Zealand, Joey leaped for the rail and missed, slipping into the sea. Sailmaker Karl Sperling and sailor Hilgard Pannes quickly launched the ship's dinghy and rowed back to where they imagined Joey might be. "The last glimpse I had of poor Joseph was when an inquiring albatross, which had been gliding around, came down near him to examine this strange object, but the cat lifted a ginger paw and smote his visitor heartily over the nose," wrote Villiers. All were losing hope after 20 minutes of searching, but suddenly the rowers saw Joey swimming toward them, and they were able to grab him and get him back to the ship. Within two days Joey was back in the rigging, but everyone noticed he had become a little more careful.

After spending several weeks at Tahiti and rounding stormy Cape Horn at the tip of South America, the *Joseph Conrad* and her cats arrived at New York in October 1936. The ship had sailed 57,800 miles in 555 days. Her cats Joseph and Conrad had sailed about 26,000 miles during their 336 days on board.

When news of their rescue of the spunky cat spread, Sperling and Pannes received medals from the Humane Society of America and the

Royal Humane Society of London for their brave devotion to Joey.

Alan Villiers sold the *Joseph Conrad* in November 1936, and for four years she served as the yacht of G. Huntington Hartford. Hartford turned her over to the U.S. Maritime Commission in 1939, and she again served as a training vessel for merchant marine sailors during World War II. In 1947, by Act of Congress, she was turned over to Mystic Seaport, where she has served as an exhibit and a stationary training vessel ever since. While she was restored recently to reflect the period just before Alan Villiers purchased her, Joey would find her decks and rigging quite familiar today.

Alan Villiers settled in England and went on to a successful career as a maritime author and expert, writing 40 books. In 1957 he was captain of the reproduction Pilgrim ship, *Mayflower II*, when she sailed from England to Plymouth, Massachusetts. He visited his old ship at Mystic Seaport several times before his death in 1982.

Artist Victor J. Dowling, who turned Joey into such an engaging character, was born in 1906 and grew up in the Bronx, New York. From an early age, he loved to write stories and draw pictures. His family spent their summers on farms in New York State and sometimes vacationed at the shore, but, so far as we know, he was never a sailor like Alan Villiers and Joey.

Victor Dowling attended the College of the Holy Cross, in Worcester, Massachusetts, and then studied at the National Academy of Design Art Schools, where he won a medal for drawing the human figure. Animals—cats and chickens in particular—remained his favorite subject, however, and the first picture he ever sold was a portrait of two cats for the *Herald Tribune Sunday Magazine*. He went on to illustrate over 30 books and many articles and stories. *Joey Goes to Sea*, published in 1939, was his first book. One of his later books, *Mr. Cat*, written by actor George Freedly and published in 1960, became a national bestseller.

The Dowling family had moved to their own farm in East Taghkanic, New York, in 1934. There Victor and his brother Robert raised chickens and kept all sorts of pets, from dogs and donkeys to an opossum. Victor also taught art classes and was a justice of the peace. He later completed law school in Albany and was admitted to the New York State bar shortly before his death in 1963.

And Joey? As described here, after squeezing the experiences of nearly nine cat's lives into his eleven months at sea, he was adopted and taken to a quiet home in Philadelphia. Writing three years after their return, Villiers said, "I wish I could take Joey with me on another voyage, but it would be too bad to take him away from his good home in Philadelphia."

Captain Alan Villiers, with a camera on board his ship, the *Joseph Conrad*. Photo by Hans Christian Petersen. (Zangenberg Collection, Mystic Seaport, 1988-10-111)

If you liked *Joey Goes to Sea* you might enjoy these other books from Mystic Seaport.

Nora the Fifty-Cent Dog is written and illustrated by Lolly Stoddard. Adopted by a Coast Guardsman, Nora—a German Shepherd—served in the U.S. Coast Guard Beach Patrol on North Carolina's Outer Banks during World War II. When her master faints during a November storm on the beach, Nora saves him from death and beocmes a celebrity—the fifty-cent dog who made good defending her country and its servicemen.

32 pages, 15 illustrations, ISBN 0-939510-87-1 (paper) $9.95
ISBN 0-939510-88-X (hardbound) $15.50

Town Small, written and illustrated by Lolly Stoddard, is a charming look at a coastal community and its busy seasons. Read along as this little seaside town fills with summer visitors and boats, and the drawbridge goes up and down at the heart of town.

32 pages, 17 illustrations, ISBN 0-939510-77-4 (paper) $9.95

What is a Sea Dog?, written by John Jensen and illustrated by Richard J. King, is inspired by the exhibit *Sea Dogs! Great Tails of the Sea*, at Mystic Seaport. Join little Skipper, a curious puppy in an orange life preserver, as she meets a galaxy of sea dogs from past and present. *What is a Sea Dog?* combines poetry, history, and fun in a celebration of the many dogs who love the water.

24 pages, 27 illustrations, ISBN 0-939510-81-2 (paper) $4.95

Mystic Seaport—The Museum of America and the Sea—is the nation's leading maritime museum, presenting the American experience from a maritime perspective. Located along the banks of the historic Mystic River in Mystic, Connecticut, the Museum houses extensive collections representing the material culture of maritime America, and offers educational programs from preschool to postgraduate.

For more information, call us at 888-9SEAPORT, or visit us on the Web at *www.mysticseaport.org*